WELCOME TO

Ballet School

Frances Lincoln
Children's Books

Dear Students!

My name is Ashley Bouder and I am a principal ballerina.

My aim with this book is to inspire you to believe that ballet can let you be anything. There are all sorts of characters and things we can play with using our ballet technique.

I created the characters and story to show you that no matter what you look like, ballet is for everyone!

Miss Marcia is inspired by my real life ballet teacher Marcia Dale Weary. She instilled not only a solid ballet technique, but a deep passion for the arts and life in me. She dedicated her life to training young ballet dancers and her "children" dance all over the world. I love her.

I encourage you to read the story and try out the moves on each page in front of the mirror. Maybe even put on a little show at the end to some music.

My favorite character to dance from Sleeping Beauty is Aurora. I can't wait to hear what yours is. Turn the page and enter the magical world of ballet!

A.B.

"Welcome to your first day at ballet school!
I am Miss Marcia and I will be your teacher.
Hurry up little ones! Say goodbye and come
on in. Let's get ready for class."

"What color tights, leotard, or T-shirt will you choose to put on today for your first ballet lesson?

Make sure your hair is pulled back securely, and you have your ballet slippers ready."

"Welcome to the studio! Ballet is the most beautiful way of dancing. It requires strength and grace. It is also a way to tell stories without words. I can't wait to share it with you. Everyone, put on your ballet slippers! Let's warm up and introduce ourselves."

AMIRAH

ALEJANDRO

VIOLET

Warm-ups and Stretching

"To get our bodies warmed up and ready to dance, let's start with some simple head rolls.

First we roll to the right...

... then to the left.

Next, we roll our shoulders forward and back to warm up more muscles.

Now, we move onto rolling
our ankles one way, then
the other.

We can extend our arms and
circle our wrists, then swing
our arms in big circles.

And finally, we are ready to learn some ballet."

The Five Positions (legs)

"Today we will learn the five basic positions for our feet and arms. Knowing these positions allows us to link ballet steps together to make a dance.

Our toes are always pointed outwards—we call this TURNOUT—and our knees are always pulled up and straight in our positions.

Since there are five of you, everyone pick a position to try."

FIRST POSITION

"Heels together, toes pointed out!"

SECOND POSITION

"Separate the feet to the side."

THIRD POSITION

"Cross one foot halfway across the other."

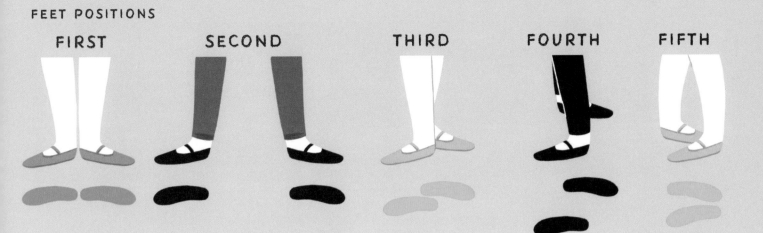

FIRST   SECOND   THIRD   FOURTH   FIFTH

FOURTH POSITION

"Separate the feet front to back!"

FIFTH POSITION

"Cross one foot over the other completely."

The Five Positions (arms)

"Wonderful! Now let's try the five arm positions. Your arms are your wings in ballet.

They help with balance and co-ordination, but they also help you to finish a movement beautifully. Hold them up using your back."

FIRST POSITION

"Arms in front, gently bent at the elbow. Palms facing in."

SECOND POSITION

"Open both arms to the side. They should be slightly curved forwards. Take care **not** to throw them out fully into a T-shape."

THIRD POSITION

"Combine the first and second positions. One arm in front, one arm to the side."

FIFTH POSITION

"Both arms evenly rounded above your head. Grow tall and reach for the sky!"

FOURTH POSITION

"One arm in first and one arm raised above your head. Keep your shoulders down."

HAND POSITION

"Shake and relax your hand. Stretch out your index (first) and little fingers as far as possible. Pull in your thumb underneath."

"Now we know all the arm and leg positions, let's try them together! Remember to extend your arms all the way to your fingertips and don't forget your wrists. They should be lifted. Your shoulders should always be pressed down. Don't let them creep up!"

At the Barre: Learning the Steps

"Now that we have our basic positions, let's learn some real ballet steps. All ballet steps have names in French because France is where the art of ballet was invented. We always begin ballet class by holding on to the barre. Let's learn some basic ballet step positions."

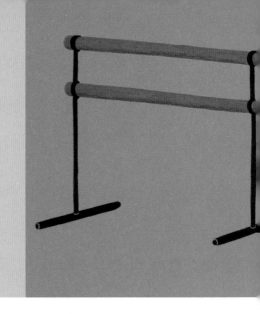

PLIÉ

"Bend your knees"

TENDU

"Stretch your leg"

PLIÉ means bent, so we bend our knees. We can plié in all five foot positions and even with one foot off the ground, which we will practice later.

TENDU means to stretch, so we stretch our leg pointi our toes and keeping them on the floor. Like many ballet steps, a tendu can be to the front, side, or bac

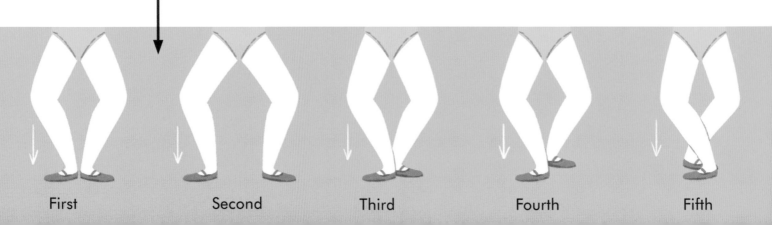

First   Second   Third   Fourth   Fifth

First Second Third Fourth Fifth

RELEVÉ

RELEVÉ means raised, so we raise just our heels off the floor and go onto tiptoe. We can relevé in all five foot positions or with one leg off the ground too!

DÉGAGÉ

"Lift your toes"

"Heels raised"

DÉGAGÉ means disengaged, so we begin like we are doing a tendu from fifth position, but we lift our toes off the floor a little bit.

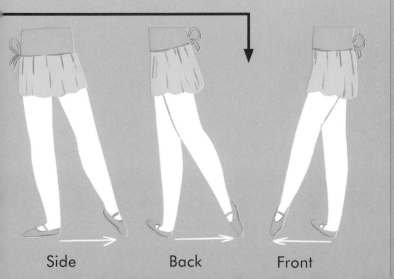

Side Back Front

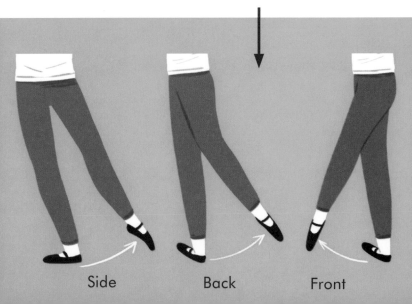

Side Back Front

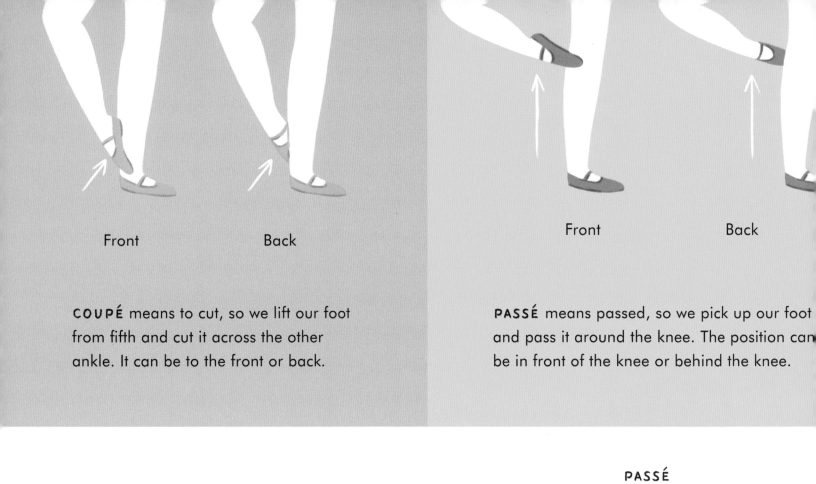

Front   Back

Front   Back

COUPÉ means to cut, so we lift our foot from fifth and cut it across the other ankle. It can be to the front or back.

PASSÉ means passed, so we pick up our foot and pass it around the knee. The position can be in front of the knee or behind the knee.

COUPÉ

PASSÉ

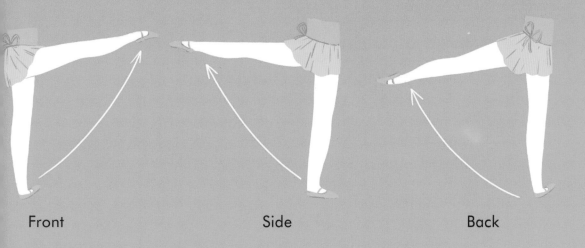

Front Side Back

GRAND BATTEMENT means big beat, so we kick our legs as high as we can and close our feet back into fifth position. This step can also be done front, side, or back.

ATTITUDE

GRAND BATTEMENT

ATTITUDE is a position of the leg in the air, when it is bent at an angle. It is usually done to the front or back, but can be done to the side too.

Front Side

Back

"Well done everyone! Now let's use these basic steps to do some more complicated moves that we often see in dances."

FONDU means melted. We start in fifth, then we coupé with our standing leg in plié. Then we extend our leg to dégagé position.

FONDU

Fifth   Coupé   Plié   Extend   Dégagé

FRAPPÉ means struck. Starting in coupé, we hit the floor on our way to dégagé.

FRAPPÉ

Fifth   Coupé   *Strike*   Dégagé   *Strike*   Coupé

DÉVELOPPÉ means develop, so we open out and unfold our leg as high as we can. Again, we start in fifth, go through COUPÉ to PASSÉ to ATTITUDE and then continue to straighten our leg up. Then we TENDU on the floor and close back to fifth. It can be done to the front, side, or back. When the leg is to the back, it is called ARABESQUE.

FIFTH

PASSÉ

ATTITUDE

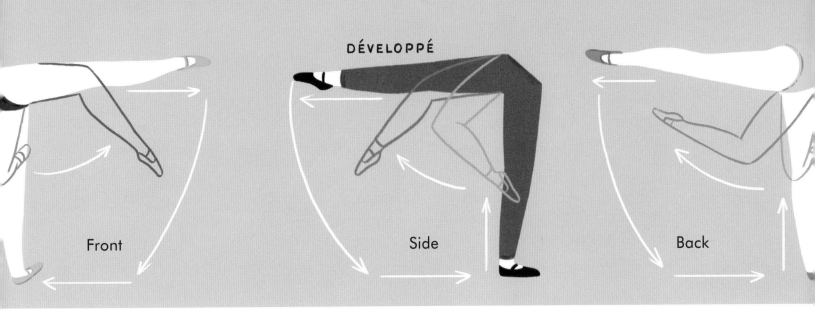

DÉVELOPPÉ

Front

Side

Back

DÉVELOPPÉ

TENDU

"The GRAND BATTEMENT usually ends our barre practice. Before we move to center, can I have a brave volunteer to touch my hands with their toes in grand battement?

Great, thank you Violet! Now, show me your highest grand battement..."

It's okay little ballerina! It is better to try our hardest and fall down than to not try at all. We will try again tomorrow.

"Now everyone, let's move to the center of the room.

Alejandro, help me demonstrate how to do a turn. In ballet the word for turn is PIROUETTE. To do a basic pirouette, we start in fifth position. First we tendu side. Then we rond de jambe our leg to fourth in plié. Next, we push off with our back leg to turn towards that leg in passé. When we have finished a whole turn we close back to fifth position.

TENDU

ROND DE JAMBE

PASSÉ

"Push off with your back leg"

"Stretch and point"

"Slide into fourth and bend your knees"

Turns can be executed to the right or the left. Ballet dancers usually prefer one side to the other. Which side do you like?"

PIROUETTE

PASSÉ

"Spin towards the raised leg"

"Passé to fifth"

"Let's move onto the final part of ballet class... JUMPING! In ballet, **SAUTÉ** means to spring or jump. We can sauté in any position. Let's everyone try a jump in their favorite position."

"I'm jumping in first position..." – **AMIRAH**

"I'm jumping in an arabesque." – **VIOLET**

"I'm jumping in passé." – **JOONWON**

"I'm jumping in attitude front!" – SAHANI

"... and I'm finishing with a grand jeté!" – AMIRAH

"I'm jumping in coupé back." – ALEJANDRO

"The last step of the day is the grand jeté. It means big throw, so we jump up as high as we can and throw our legs into a split in the air. The arms can be in different positions. It makes the dancer look like they are flying across the stage!"

"Now it is time to end our class. We finish with RÉVÉRENCE, which means bow. At the end of class, we bow to our teacher in thanks for the instruction and knowledge. In a performance, we thank the audience for coming to watch us with our bows."

"There are different ways to bow.
Everyone pick their favorite!"

Storytime: Sleeping Beauty

"Thank you everyone! Now that we know some ballet
steps, I'd like to invite a guest to help us with a famous
ballet story…. Violet's mom! I used to teach her when she
was your age. She has danced Sleeping Beauty on stage
and has some tips for us."

"Hello class! Let's pick out our favorite scenes and characters
from Sleeping Beauty and put our new ballet steps into action.
Remember, ballet is a way to tell stories without words."

"Once upon a time in a faraway magical kingdom, a baby princess was born. Her name was Aurora and she had six fairy protectors, each with a quality to bestow upon the princess at her christening.

So let's start with the five fairies here! Wands everyone!
Cast a spell on the princess. Pick a pose that best fits your gift."

"The orange fairy gives Aurora tenderness. I'm gracefully moving my leg into passé to show beauty and kindness." - SAHANI

"The blue fairy gives Aurora vivacity. I'm showing energy with a dégagé side." – JOONWON

"The pink fairy gives Aurora courage. I'm going to jump in attitude to fly through the air." – VIOLET

"The yellow fairy gives Aurora eloquence. I'm doing a tendu back to show an elegant line." – ALEJANDRO

"The green fairy gives Aurora generosity. I'm extending my arms and doing an attitude side to show openness." – AMIRAH

"But before the Lilac Fairy could give her gift to the princess, another fairy arrived. It was the evil fairy Carabosse, who had been left off the guest list. She stormed into the castle and put a curse on the baby. When Princess Aurora turned sixteen, she would prick her finger on a spindle and die. *Gasp!* It was a good thing the Lilac Fairy still had her gift to give the princess. The Lilac Fairy bravely faced Carabosse and changed her spell to ensure Aurora would not die, but that she and the rest of the kingdom would fall into a deep sleep."

"Carabosse, run around the room once. Look disgustedly at the fairies."

"She proclaimed that one day the kiss of true love from a handsome prince would wake Aurora and kingdom. Knowing she had been thwarted, Carabosse fled the castle. And the kingdom went about getting rid of all spindles, in order to ensure Aurora's safety."

"Let's choose our characters! Carabosse or the Lilac Fairy? Carabosse delights in being evil. The Lilac Fairy is goodness and light."

"Lilac Fairies, you need to tell Carabosse to leave. Shake your head 'no' and use your arms to show Carabosse where to go."

"Carabosse, shrink back. Use your face to tell the story."

"Sixteen years later, there was an enormous celebration for Aurora's birthday. The whole kingdom was invited and four suitors from far away lands attended to try to win Aurora's hand in marriage. The princess danced the Rose Adagio with the suitors, in which each gave her a rose to capture her heart."

"Who wants to play Aurora at her sixteenth birthday? Thank you Amirah. And then the rest of you can play her suitors. This is one of the most famous dances in Sleeping Beauty, the Rose Adagio."

"Joonwon, support her with your hand and walk her around in a circle."

"Keep your chest up in attitude, Amirah. Balance on your tiptoe. This is one of the most difficult parts in the ballet. Good!"

"Everyone else, you should be proudly waiting for your dance with Aurora."

"Before Aurora could choose, an old woman arrived and presented her with a whole bouquet of flowers. Happily, the princess took the bunch and began to dance with them. As she was dancing, she hugged the flowers, then threw them and gasped. She looked at her finger, while her father took the flowers and pulled out a spindle. It was Carabosse's spell!"

"Lilac Fairy, cast your sleep spell on the kingdom."

"Carabosse, laugh at your own trick and run offstage."

MWAHAHAH

"Suddenly Carabosse appears to gloat and laugh at the King and Queen. They are fearful, but then the Lilac Fairy appears. She gently reminds everyone about her counter spell. As soon as Aurora is safely tucked into her bed, the Lilac Fairy puts the rest of the kingdom to sleep to await the arrival of a prince."

"I need a Carabosse, Lilac Fairy, Aurora, and some suitors here."

"Everyone else, peacefully fall to the floor asleep."

"One hundred years later, the handsome Prince Desiré is wandering alone in the forest, when he comes upon the Lilac Fairy, who has been waiting for him. By this time Aurora's kingdom is covered in large thorny vines. The Lilac Fairy tells the prince of the horrible spell placed upon the beautiful princess who lays inside. To convince the reluctant prince, the Lilac Fairy shows him a vision of Aurora."

"Who wants to be a prince? And the Lilac Fairy? Thank you Violet and Alejandro. Let's act out the Lilac Fairy's vision of Aurora."

GASP

"Lilac Fairy, you need to show the prince a vision of Aurora: use your arms to show the prince where to look. Prince, you should look shocked."

"Aurora, remember to turn your hip and leg out."

"Believing the Lilac Fairy, the prince sets about cutting through all the vines. Finally, he gets to the castle door and enters to search for the Princess Aurora. Finding her asleep, he bends down and places the softest of kisses on her lips."

"Lilac Fairy, show the prince where Aurora is, using your arms."

"Prince! Wake Aurora up by blowing a kiss."

"At once, the princess wakes, breaking the spell and getting rid of Carabosse for good. The entire kingdom also wakes. Having fallen in love with the princess at first sight, the prince immediately asks for Aurora's hand in marriage. The king, queen, and the Lilac Fairy all give their blessings."

"This is a really big scene where the princess wakes!"

"Aurora, stretch and yawn to show you are waking up!"

"Carabosse, use your facial expression to look angry and defeated."

"Princess Aurora and Prince Desiré's wedding is magnificent. All of the courtiers are invited, as well as some special guests, who perform dances in honor of the couple. The special guests are the White Cat and Puss in Boots, Princess Florine and her Bluebird, Red Riding Hood and the Wolf, and some acrobatic Jesters."

"We start in fifth position plié."

"Lift our back leg to passé."

"Then we jump in the air putting both legs in passé."

"So let's learn one more jumping ballet step, so we can all play either the White Cat or Puss in Boots. In ballet, some steps are named after animals. If we lift one bent leg up to one side, then jump and lift the other, that is a PAS DE CHAT. We can do many in a row, or just one."

"This is my favorite move."–
JOONWON

"We land with the second leg still in passé."

"Then we close that foot front to fifth position in plié."

"Now let's all put on our blue feathers and fly like Bluebird from the wedding scene! We can do all the jumps we learned today and flap our arms at the same time to look like a bird."

"Beautiful jumping everyone!"

"The wedding ends with the crowning of the prince and
princess, and they live happily ever after."

"Okay everyone—let's get ready for a special performance to our loved ones. Let's show them everything we learned today! Pick out your costumes and your favorite color tutus. Pin back your hair and paint your faces. Gather your props and masks. Your stage call is 5 minutes until the curtain goes up!"

"I'm going to be the LILAC FAIRY."

"I'm PRINCE DESIRÉ!"

"Thank you everyone for a wonderful day! I hope that you enjoyed the lessons and will come back soon. Remember, ballet is one of the best ways to express ourselves without words. It is an art form but requires an athlete to perform the steps. Take inspiration from these great dancers on the wall. You are all off to a good start!"

Megan Fairchild

Lauren Cuthbertson

Isaac Hernández

Kimin Kim

Elisa Carrillo Cabrera

Steven McRae

Albert Evans

Yuan Yuan Tan

Michaela DePrince

Joaquín De Luz

Tamara Rojo

Glossary

ARABESQUE — a position on one leg with the other behind, either on the ground or in the air

À TERRE — the leg is on the ground

ATTITUDE — standing on one leg with the other lifted. The leg in the air is bent at the knee.

CHAÎNÉ — "chains." A series of short, rapid turns performed in a straight line across the floor

COUPÉ — to cut

CROISÉ — crossed

DÉGAGÉ — "to disengage." Dégagé is a movement where the working leg "disengages" from the supporting leg.

DÉVELOPPÉ — to develop

EN BAS — low

EN DEDANS — inwards

EN DEHORS — outwards

EN L'AIR — in the air

ÉPAULEMENT — the position of the head, neck, and shoulders

FONDU — melting or sinking down

FRAPPÉ — to strike

GRAND BATTEMENT — big beat

JETÉ — to throw

SAUTÉ — to spring or jump

PAS DE CHAT — "step of the cat." A jump from fifth to fifth with an overlapping action with each leg bending and unfurling

PASSÉ — to pass

PIROUETTE — a turn balanced on one foot

PLIÉ — to bend

PORT DE BRAS — movement of the arms from one position to another

RELEVÉ — to rise with a small rising action onto your toes, with bent knees

RÉVÉRENCE — a bow or curtsy to pay respect to the teacher or thank the audience

ROND DE JAMBE — circling action of the leg on the floor

TENDU — to stretch (an extending action of the leg)

This book is dedicated to the loving memory of the great Marcia Dale Weary and the student she never had, Violet Storm. Marcia's legacy will touch her all the same. — A. B.

For my grandmother, Margarita. — J. B.

Q Quarto Knows

Inspiring | Educating | Creating | Entertaining

Brimming with creative inspiration, how-to projects, and useful information to enrich your everyday life, Quarto Knows is a favorite destination for those pursuing their interests and passions. Visit our site and dig deeper with our books into your area of interest: Quarto Creates, Quarto Cooks, Quarto Homes, Quarto Lives, Quarto Drives, Quarto Explores, Quarto Gifts, or Quarto Kids.

Ballet School © 2020 Quarto Publishing plc. Text © 2020 Ashley Bouder. Illustrations © 2020 Julia Bereciartu
First Published in 2020 by Frances Lincoln Children's Books,
an imprint of The Quarto Group. Quarto Boston North Shore, 100 Cummings Center, Suite 265D, Beverly, MA 01915, USA. Tel: +1 978-282-9590
Fax: +1 978-283-2742 **www.QuartoKnows.com**

The right of Ashley Bouder to be identified as the illustrator and Julia Bereciartu to be identified as the author of this work has been asserted by them in accordance with the Copyright, Designs and Patents Act, 1988 (United Kingdom).

A catalogue record for this book is available from the British Library.

ISBN 978-0-7112-5128-1 (US edition)

The illustrations were created in gouache and colored pencils.
Set in Mrs Green, Futura, Raindrop, Palomino Sans
Published by Katie Cotton
Designed by Karissa Santos
Edited by Katy Flint
Production by Caragh McAleenan
Manufactured in China 052020
9 8 7 6 5 4 3 2 1

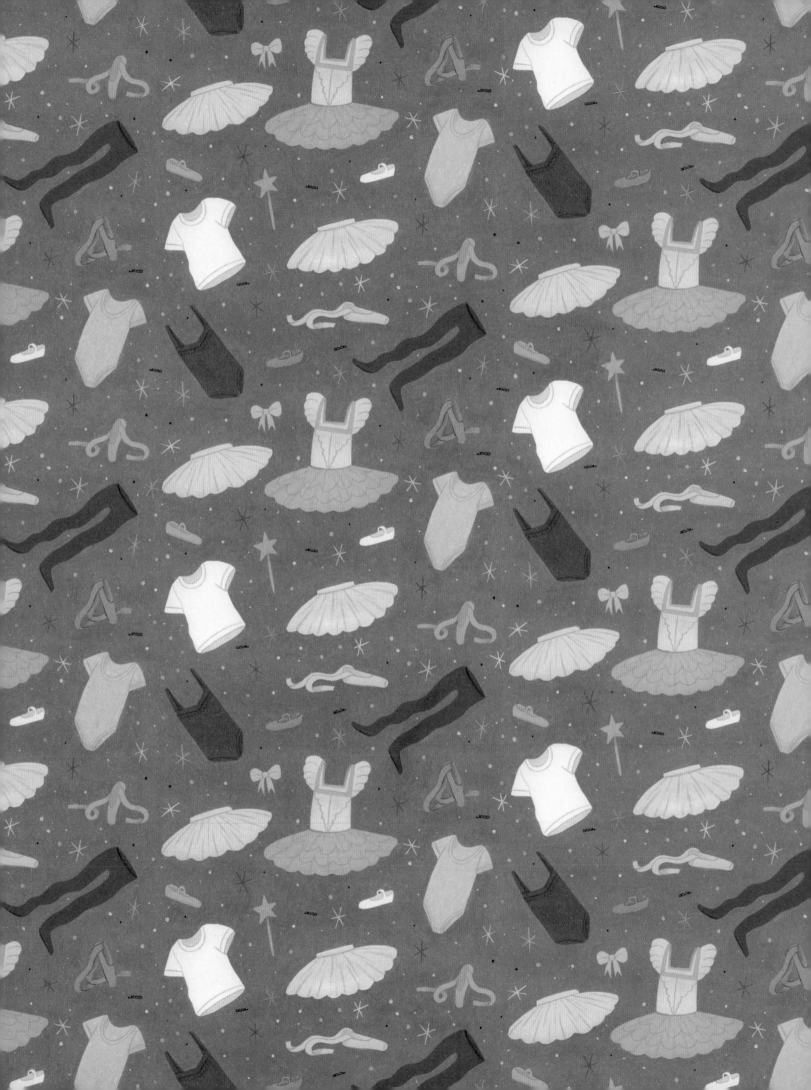